SEASONS & SONS

The Reforming Role of Spiritual Sons

Dr. Paul Crites

Seasons & Sons: The Reforming Role of Spiritual Sons
Copyright © 2019 by Paul Crites
All rights reserved

Unless otherwise indicated, all Scripture quotations are taken from the New King James Version of the Bible.

No part of this book may be reproduced or stored in a retrieval system, or transmitted in any form or by any means, electronic, mechanical, photocopying, recording, or otherwise without the express written permission of the publisher.

Published by RevMedia Publishing
PO Box 5172
Kingwood, TX 77325

ISBN 978-1-7324922-7-1
Printed in the United States of America

Thank You to the following for helping make this book a reality: Dr. Ben Klynhans for his incredible fathering insight and teaching, Robert Mickey, my son, friend and editor and all of my sons who have made me the father I am today.

TABLE OF CONTENTS

1. A SEASON EASILY MISSED — 13
2. A SEASON OF DIVINE ORDER AND SEQUENCE — 17
3. A SEASON OF AWAKENING — 21
4. A SEASON OF KINGDOM PROXIMITY — 27
5. A SEASON OF UNITY — 33
6. A SEASON OF FINDING YOUR AUTHENTIC VOICE — 37
7. A SEASON OF OBEDIENCE — 41
8. A SEASON OF ORDER — 47
9. A SEASON OF GREAT OPPORTUNITY — 53
10. THE SEASON OF HONOR — 59

WHY I WROTE THIS BOOK

Joshua chapter three records that what previously had taken forty years, was now happening in just three days.

Moses had led them out.

Joshua was going to bring them in.

A New Season was upon them.

A Son was leading them. A confident, mature son.

The purpose of a New Season is the restoration of biblical truth.

"Early in the morning Joshua and all the Israelites set out from Shittim and went to the Jordan, where they camped before crossing over. After three days the officers went throughout the camp, giving orders to the people: "When you see the ark of the covenant of the Lord your God, and the Levitical priests carrying it, you are to move out from your positions and follow it. Then you will know which way to go, **since you have never been this way before...**" *Joshua 3:1-4*

We have entered into a New Season.

A Season of Sons who are maturing under true fathers in the Lord. Just as Joshua told the people, "you have never been this way before," we cannot operate in this new season with old paradigms or perspectives obtained through past experiences.

We are moving into new, uncharted territory.

It's a season of new influence.

There is revealed truth from the past seasons that remains of great value. However reviving traditions and nonbiblical methods must end. We do not need another "revival."

A reformation is required.

Every New Season must give way to a new wineskin, lest the old wineskin implodes and the new wine is lost. The new wineskin in this season is the restoration of God's family and order in the earth. It is birthed with the voice of a Spiritual father with the goal of maturing sons.

(Note: Reference to sons includes men & women)

For Sons to mature they will need to recognize, submit and learn from the Spiritual Father God has sent them.

This book is for you to know a key truth in this Season.

Many leaders in past generations were never fathered. Thus, personalities replaced principles; equipping was replaced with entertaining and gifting and skills replaced character and honor.

There is a new generation hungry for truth. They desperately desire to see how a functional family operates.

When the Father saw the earth was out of order, He sowed His Son and reaped a family.

God's family here on earth desperately needs fathers to mature sons.

We read the last verse of the Old Covenant in Malachi 4:6 as a direct message to this season.

And he will turn he hearts of the fathers to the children, and the hearts of the children to their fathers, lest I come and strike the earth with a curse.

Adam became both spiritually and naturally an orphan. Through his action, he orphaned the entire human race.

Orphans lack identity.

Identity comes through a father.

Jesus said, if you have seen me, you have seen the Father, if you have heard me you have heard the Father. John 14:9

Jesus is the biblical model to manifest the Father's will on earth as it is in heaven. This is the time and season all creation has awaited. The revealing of His sons.

For the earnest expectation of the creation eagerly waits for the revealing of the sons of God. Rom.8:19

As the Olympic runner in the final lap of the relay race, the Spiritual son must not lag behind or run ahead of his Spiritual father. No, he must pace himself for the perfect moment of the handing off of the baton in order to successfully run the race and introduce the new season.

CHAPTER ONE

A SEASON EASILY MISSED

People are desperate for a roadmap in this New Season.

If you aren't careful, you can miss it.

Somehow the biblical blueprint for the church has changed over the years. We have become a reactive people focused on everything from generational curses to an overly sensitive, offended, weak group of people.

Major books have been written on "How Not to be Offended."

How sad that the people of God who once stood with heads held high in Rome while being fed to lions, now must be reminded and taught how not to be offended.

God's order in the earth of fathers and sons has been replaced with pastors, boards and members. Despite satellites broadcasting 24-7, massive publishing houses and churches on every corner, the lack of biblical order and spiritual growth is evident.

We must return to the Designer's manual, the Bible.

We must return to the biblical pattern for success and influence through the teaching of fathers and sons.

It is extremely important you don't miss this new season.

If you don't recognize it, you will miss it; or worse yet, buy into a counterfeit.

For example, John the Baptist was the forerunner of Jesus.

He was crying in the wilderness and told everyone, there is One coming and when He gets here, everything is going to change. I'm not even worthy to untie His sandals.

Suddenly, one day Jesus emerged out of the crowd to be baptized.

John baptized Jesus and the heavens opened and the Father spoke saying, "This is My Son Whom I am well pleased."

The Father affirmed His Son.

That's what fathers do.

Jesus came out of the Jordan River after John baptized Him and went into a temple. What is interesting is that John the Baptist didn't drop everything and follow Him.

John watched Him walk right by him and leave.

John didn't lay down his ministry.

Even though he previously gave his life to proclaim the new season that was coming, he let it walk right past him and he held onto the old season.

In fact, the Bible states that when John was in prison, he called his disciples. Instead of telling his disciples to follow Jesus, he held onto his followers.

John becomes so confused that he later calls his followers back to the prison cell and says,

"Do you think that really was the Messiah?" John 11:3

Can you imagine following God's assignment in preparing people for the next season and when it appears you miss it?

When you miss the new season, you are left wondering and in doubt.

Boldness is replaced with uncertainty.

This didn't cost John just his ministry, but his head.

What is the **key** to the new season?

Being teachable and walking in humility.

Receiving the revelation and impartation that

comes from a spiritual father in your life.

The proof that God is operating in your life is positive change.

Many are wandering around in the spiritual wilderness without recognizing the Spiritual father God has sent them. They attend church faithfully, volunteer, give offerings, pray but very little changes.

**The only changes some
see are not so good ones.**

We live in a culture critical of fathers.

The "Church" has been pampered, mothered and run on feelings and emotions for far too long.

It is the season of fathers maturing sons.

Do not permit society or religion to disconnect you from this season.

Allow the Holy Spirit to awaken you.

Do not miss this new season.

CHAPTER TWO

A SEASON OF DIVINE ORDER AND SEQUENCE

The message came forward out of John but instead of him becoming a disciple of Jesus, he watched the Son of God walk right by.

This is proof that you can be so focused on your message and method, that you don't **recognize** the change in season.

The stories of Abraham, Isaac, Jacob and Joseph, teach us about Fathers and Sons.

Joseph rises to the second in command under the Pharaoh of Egypt.

Much focus has been placed on Joseph's "pit to the palace" story. We must look closer to see the bigger picture of God's order and purpose in the father's affirmation and blessing in Genesis 47:5-10

> *Then Pharaoh said to Joseph, "Now that your father and brothers have joined you here, choose any place in the entire land of Egypt for them to live. Give them the best land of Egypt. Let them live in the region of Goshen. And if any of them*

have special skills, put them in charge of my livestock, too.

Joseph had eleven brothers but only brought **five** with him to meet the Pharaoh. Here are the five and the meaning of their names:

Reuben: Seeing

Simeon: Hearing

Levi: Joined

Benjamin: Right Hand

Issachar: Wages

Five represents **balance** and **grace**.

We have five senses, we have five fingers and five toes, we embrace the five-fold ministry and David had five smooth stones when he went up against Goliath.

It's important to recognize the balance that brothers bring.

With the right "Brothers" you can secure the best land. As a Spiritual Son the role and gifting of your brothers is important to your success.

Know your brothers giftings.

Then Joseph presented his father, Jacob to Pharaoh. And **Jacob blessed Pharaoh.**

Jacob blessed Pharaoh. Did you get that?

Shouldn't have been the other way around?

Isn't this a reversal of the principle, "the greater always blesses the lesser"?

Jacob knew his **identity**.

Abraham's blessing and favor followed Isaac.

Isaac 's blessing and favor followed Jacob.

Jacob's blessing and favor found its way to Pharaoh's palace through **his son**, Joseph.

Jacob was not moved by the splendor of Pharaoh's courts or palace. He understood Divine order and sequence.

"How old are you?" Pharaoh asked him.

Jacob replied, "I have traveled this earth for 130 hard years. But my life has been short compared to the lives of my ancestors."

Then Jacob blessed Pharaoh **again** before leaving his court.

Pharaoh is recognized as a god. There's none greater in all the land.

Jacob blesses Pharaoh in accordance with God's promise that **all** the nations of the world, including Egypt, will be blessed because of Israel.

Pharaoh's recognition of the Son received the blessing from the Father

When you walk in the blessing and favor of your Spiritual father, you have nothing to prove to anyone.

When you know who you are and walk in God's divine order, you have no contender, challenger or rival.

CHAPTER THREE
A SEASON OF AWAKENING

In Luke 15, there was a man of wealth who had two sons. The younger son asked his father for his "portion" of his inheritance before his father's death and upon receiving it, he not only leaves his home but his country.

The younger son took his **"portion."**

Unfortunately, he continued to **think** and **live** like he was still under the **covering** of his father's "unlimited resources."

He was an immature son.

He left his father's house without the father's blessing.

An immature son who refuses to listen, follow instruction and walk in order is scheduling poverty and shame in their life. (Proverbs 13:18)

To make matters worse, he connected himself to a different country (a different system), a place that didn't **recognize**/identify him or **his father**.

He lost his wealth and influence.

He no longer had unlimited resources.

He lost his portion.

He had no access to any resources.

Now he has experienced the greatest loss, his identity

This is why immature sons must **awake** and embrace this new Season.

In over forty years of ministering to people, I have painfully watched the "immature son mindset" play out over and over again.

As individuals come into the Kingdom and set themselves under the covering of a Spiritual Father's house, they learn principles that give them life and more abundant life. (John 10:10)

They embrace healing, prosperity, enjoy a blessed life and experience unlimited Kingdom resources.

Until one day, something goes wrong in their life.

In their immaturity they pack up their stuff and leave their father's house **without** the father's blessing.

They relocate over to another church (another country/system) where they have **no identity**.

They struggle, find fault or not "feel" like they fit in and move on again. They begin to believe they don't fit anywhere so they must begin their **own ministry**. They minister out of their small portion, **it's all they know**, but eventually it runs out.

No father, no identity and no access to unlimited resources.

The real issue is that they physically left the father's house but mentally they did not. They continue to function like they are in the father's house where there is an unlimited source.

But their portion has run out.

I am amazed by people who believe they can disconnect from a Spiritual father and it have no consequences.

One day, like the younger son, their portion will run out.

With his "portion" depleted, and a severe famine in the foreign country. The younger son was in serious **trouble**. He could only secure a job feeding pigs.

His lack forced him to focus on the pig's portion. However, the pigs were preferred over him.

The young son had an awakening in the pig pen.

He said to himself, 'How many of my father's hired servants have bread enough and to spare, and I perish with hunger! I will arise and go to my father, and will say to him, "Father, I have **sinned** against **heaven** and before **you**, and I am no longer worthy to be called your son. Make me like one of your **hired** servants." (Luke 15:21,22)

In his self-centered immaturity the young man came to an **Awakening**: he had sinned against **heaven** and **earth**.

Rebellion and independence always create **loss**.

The younger son identity is **lost**.

He now **sees himself** as a servant.

There is no record that the Father ever pursued or sought after his younger son.

Fathers do not **chase** sons.

When a son returns to his father's house, he must repent, listen and obey instructions.

A Father will:

Recognize a son who turns his heart toward him.

Restore a son who humbles and repents at the door of the father's house.

Reestablish an obedient son's identity in the house.

After the younger son repented, his father immediately did three things:

Covered him with the best robe.

Connected him to "unlimited supply" with a signet ring.

Confirms his identity as a son and placed shoes on his feet because servants didn't wear shoes.

During the celebration that followed, the older son became angry and judged the younger son for what "he assumed" he did. The older son announced he had followed the rules, did the right thing and no one had given him and his friends a party.

A wrong attitude can manifest from those closest to us.

A good son will support his father's decision.

The father steps outside his house to remind the older judgmental son that he has always had access to "unlimited resources." He teaches the older son that **restoring** is always the right thing to do.

The older son failed to understand that a son may leave the father's **house**, but he never leaves his **heart**.

NOTES

CHAPTER FOUR
A SEASON OF KINGDOM PROXIMITY

The Bible says that the younger son "came to his senses," he had an **"awakening"** moment. His time at **PPU** – Pig Pen University was finally over!

Whatever it took, he had to get back in **proximity** to his father.

Proximity has power and purpose in the New Season.

It's the place that holds the blessing.

im•ma•ture (adjective) not fully developed.

Remember the **purpose** of this season is to **mature sons.**

For this reason, a Spiritual father cannot be confused or identified as a "Fixer."

It's the distinct difference between **Church** and the **Kingdom**.

Sons come to Church to get something.

Sons come to the Kingdom to be something.

Proximity to revelation in this season is vitally important.

In Matthew 16, when Christ asked his disciples, "who do men say I am?"

They replied, "you're one of the prophets."

Prophets heard from God. That's all they knew.

That was the season in which they lived.

When Christ asked Peter, "who do you say that I am?" Peter responded, "You are the Christ, the Son of the living God."

Peter could have said that He was Master, or King of the Universe, or many other things but he said, "You are the Son of the Living God."

Peter's **revelation from heaven** created his **Kingdom confession.**

His confession reveals God does nothing in the earth outside the Father -Son relationship.

Jesus said to Peter, "You are blessed, for flesh and blood did not reveal this to you, but My Father who is in heaven."

Peter has now opened the revelation portal for all sons.

God no longer speaks **just** through His **prophets**

but is now speaking through a former fisherman, who is a son!

And it's this kind of **revelation, the proceeding Word** that Jesus says, "He will build His Church and the **gates** of Hell shall not prevail against it." (Matthew 16:18)

The gates of cities were places where prominent men sat, strategized and conducted business.

The gates of hell not prevailing against the church, means that the strategies and forces of darkness cannot triumph against the Church of Jesus Christ.

It was the revelation of how the Father and His Son work and how the father and sons are to operate here on earth.

What else did Jesus say to Peter that day?

"And I will give you **the keys** of the kingdom of heaven, and whatever you bind on earth will be bound in heaven, and whatever you loose on earth, will be loosed in heaven." (Matthew 16:19)

Keys represent **authority.**

Kingdom authority.

An immature son cannot have access to the Keys or he will wreck the vehicle God uses to build the Kingdom.

To produce Kingdom-minded sons there must be a

place of Kingdom proximity for revelation, impartation and accountability to a father.

That Kingdom connection is what I and many refer to as the "**Household of Faith**."

As we have therefore opportunity, let us do good unto all men, especially unto them who are of the household of faith. Galatians 6:10

Following the model of the first Apostles, who taught the Apostles doctrine, broke bread, fellowshipped and declared prayers, the house of a Spiritual father will keep you in proximity to revelation (the proceeding, now Word).

The Household of Faith is part of the new wineskin that is required in this New Season.

In order for a new wineskin to be created something must die.

The old wineskin we call "church" with a pastor and members following a focused attempt to create weekly fifty-minute service that are contemporary ("seeker sensitive" or "traditional") will not provide the proximity of Kingdom revelation, impartation and accountability.

In many places the church has become a platform for gifts. There is obviously a place for God's gifts. Previous movements created a codependency upon the "gifted." No one was maturing, only flocking for an immediate word to relieve them from their immature decisions.

Personal ambition, pride and performers have replaced equipping fathers. This old wine skin must die for the new wineskin to hold the new wine.

That is why the talented orphans coming to our "churches" simply desire a quick fixer not a father. When they get their "fix" they are gone.

We must rediscover the spiritual family that the Son of God birthed in the earth and restore the biblical model of the Acts of the Apostles and Apostolic fathers.

Let us move away from a ministry conformed to this world, continuing to perform and entertain an ever-cycling circle of seekers, soakers and the religious insensitive.

True sons and daughters, who hunger to know **honor**, **identity** and **purpose**, are coming to hear the proceeding Word of impartation from a Spiritual Father.

Some are patiently awaiting the arrival of a father, one who will accept, love and receive them into his house.

When I birthed my Household of Faith in St. Augustine, Florida, I heard, "Where have you been?"

Many come with an orphan spirit, hurt, rejected, angry while others arrive ready to listen, learn and be established.

As a father, I must have this daily goal:

Always be looking for those who are looking for me.

A father must understand that many in your town will find a place in your heart before they become established in your house. Love them. Listen to them and laugh with them. Dysfunctional fathers and churches have done some damage. However, it is nothing that the Holy Spirit can not heal and bring into proper alignment.

Kingdom proximity is vital to the voice and proceeding Word you are hearing in this season. Its important in this season that you are established in a Household of Faith. It's vitally important you prioritize your time to be in proximity to your Spiritual Father's voice.

CHAPTER FIVE

A SEASON OF UNITY

King David was the second king of Israel. He ascended from a shepherd, psalmist and warrior to expand his kingdom.

King David's life as a father was painful.

Conspiracy, betrayal, murder and even civil war with his son, Absalom followed the famous king into the final days of his forty – year, generational reign.

How could Absalom and Solomon have the same father?

How could they grow up in the same house?

Absalom was a rebel focused on disunity, disagreement and dishonor.

Solomon's focus was that of unity.

Unity is where the Lord commands the blessing.

Psalm 133 states,

"Behold, how good and how pleasant it is for brethren to dwell together in unity! It is like the precious ointment upon the head, that ran down upon the beard, even Aaron's beard: that went down to the skirts of his garments; As the dew of Hermon, and as the dew that descended upon the mountains of Zion: for there the Lord commanded the blessing, even life for evermore."

The greatest desire of a Father is unity.

A divided home cannot stand. In Mark 3:25, Jesus states, *"And if a house be divided against itself, that house cannot stand."*

Your marriage, family, ministry or business cannot succeed without unity.

Unity in the Father's house creates the oil, the anointing, the corporate vessel where God commands the blessing to flow.

A unified house is the only place where an orphan spirit can receive total healing. It's the only place the hurting can lay down rejection, false identity, ambition and pride and say, "I want in this blessing."

A unified house attracts the right people at the right time and it repels those who have a divisive spirit. My tears and years have taught me a person with a divisive spirit cannot stay in a unified environment.

In the old season the attraction was the "big name

or big ministry." The new wineskin is "unity and family" because that is where God commands the blessing.

David was a man after God's heart.

David therefore departed from there and escaped to the cave of Adullam. So, when his brothers and all his father's house heard it, they went down there to him. ***And everyone who was in distress, everyone who was in debt, and everyone who was discontented gathered to him.*** *So, he became captain over them. And there were about four hundred men with him.* 1Samuel 22:1,2.

Please try to picture this: King Saul and his army are chasing David and trying to kill him.

David goes hiding in a cave.

David cries out to God to help him, and whom does God send to him?

Hundreds in debt, distress and discontented.

It does not matter a cave or a castle, a father carries an impartation that births destiny in those who are in proximity of his voice.

Now here's the powerful reality of unity.

**Those who went in the cave
with David came out differently.**

The scriptures tell us something happened under David's unifying impartation and anointing.

They were transformed.

Second Samuel 23 records that in a few years, David's men at the cave of Adullam went from being discontented, discouraged and indebted to being legendary fighting men known as **David's Mighty Men.**

Solomon, his brothers and four hundred men in a cave **recognized** and **received** in David what Absalom **refused** to acknowledge and **accept.**

In this New Season gathering together in unity is so important. Watch those who create obstacles and act contrary to what you have learned.

I urge you, brothers and sisters, to keep your eyes on those who cause dissensions and create obstacles or introduce temptations [for others] to commit sin, [acting in ways] contrary to the doctrine which you have learned. **Turn away from them.** Romans 16:17 AMP.

Guard the unity of the House.

CHAPTER SIX

A SEASON OF FINDING YOUR AUTHENTIC VOICE

When you find your voice, the right people will find you.

The voice of God is the sound of many waters.

There are many dimensions to being a mature son. God is preparing you for something greater than success, it's called significance.

Don't let anyone or anything discourage you.

There is nothing more dangerous to the enemy than someone who knows their identity and authentic voice. God wants to release a sound in you and He awakens you to a Spiritual Father to accomplish that.

A mature son will have a mature message.

A proceeding Word.

A Now Word, not a distant echo.

Time is what is required to develop your voice.

A Spiritual Father desires to see his sons maximize their sounds in the earth.

Sons must hear the sound of their Spiritual Father.

Apostles have sounds of order, prophets have directional sounds, teachers have instructional sounds, pastors have sounds of protection, and evangelists have sounds of freedom. The Spiritual Father shapes the voice of their sons.

They confirm, they rebuke and they refine their spiritual sons voice.

You give a Spiritual Father Permission to tell you No.

This is critical for the development of your voice.

Your father is cheering for you, but he's not a cheerleader, he's your coach.

Fathers teach, correct and refine including the ability to deny your access to something.

As a son you must know and appreciate that timing is everything.

If you, as a son, abandon the relationship because of your father saying no, it's obvious you didn't understand this season, covenant, or depth of relationship.

Or perhaps your mother never told you "No." Your soul may sting at the sound of "No."

However, a good Spiritual Father says "No" when it is necessary, no matter how the son responds.

A healthy family is a great place to develop and mature your voice.

In a healthy family, everyone has permission to find their voice. In a Household of Faith, you will hear and learn the voice of obedience, servanthood and honor.

There's no greater honor than to be asked to speak at your father's house.

A mature son's voice can be sent to encourage and exhort others.

For this reason, I have sent to you Timothy, my son whom I love, who is faithful in the Lord. He will remind you of my way of life in Christ Jesus, which agrees with what I teach everywhere in every church. 1Corinthians 4:17 NIV

In the old wineskin, people who had a voice or a revelation just "went." Their gifting, talent and skill opened doors.

In the New Season wineskin, a father sends his son because he knows what he has imparted into his son's voice and message.

*I hope in the Lord Jesus to **send Timothy** to you soon, that I also may be cheered when I receive news about you. I have no one else like him, who will show genuine concern for your welfare.* ***For everyone looks out for their own interests,*** *not those of Jesus Christ. But you know that Timothy has proved himself, **because as a son with his father he has served with me in the work of the gospel.** I hope, therefore, to send him as soon as I see how things go with me.* Philippians 2:19-23 NIV

In the old season everyone just went.

Very few were sent.

Why?

They did what was right in their own eyes.

Where there are no fathers, there is no authority in the house.

It's what Paul told Timothy, "everyone looks out for their own interests, not those of Jesus Christ."

In those days there was no king in Israel, but every man did that which was right in his own eyes. Judges 17:6

There must be a kingdom mandate with apostolic clarity and function. It all aligns with an authentic voice of a father.

The Apostle John wrote in his letter to his spiritual son, Gaius *"I have no greater joy than this, to hear, that my spiritual children are living (their lives) in the truth."* 3 John 4 AMP

In this new Season, your father wants you to find your authentic voice. He desires for you to walk in purpose and identity.

CHAPTER SEVEN

A SEASON OF OBEDIENCE

No one naturally obeys.

It requires reinforcement.

In this New Season obedience becomes pleasurable.

A true Spiritual son obeys his Spiritual father from a place of honor.

A Son can't wait to hear the next instruction from his Spiritual father.

Elijah and Elisha are two of the most notable prophets found in the Bible. Elijah's victory over the prophets of Baal when he called down fire from heaven was legendary. Elijah passes by Shaphat's farm near the Jordan River where Shaphat's son, Elisha was working the fields.

So, he departed from there, and found Elisha the son of Shaphat, who was plowing with twelve yokes of oxen before him, and he was with the twelfth. Then Elijah passed by him and threw his mantle on him. And he left the oxen and ran after Elijah, and said, "Please let me kiss my father

and my mother, and then I will follow you." And he said to him, "Go back again, for what have I done to you?" So, Elisha turned back from him, and took a yoke of oxen and slaughtered them and boiled their flesh, using the oxen's equipment, and gave it to the people, and they ate. Then he arose and followed Elijah, and became his servant.
1 Kings 19:19

Elisha is plowing with twelve pair of oxen, that's twenty- four oxen. Oxen were like cars, the average middle-class family had one. Just one. Elisha's family was wealthy.

Elijah is looking for a spiritual son.

Elisha must have been looking for Elijah. When Elijah threw his cloak, representing his mantle upon Elisha he reacted.

Elijah asked, do you know what I've done to you?"

A decision is required when a Spiritual father shows up.

Elisha had to decide, do I stay with what I know?

Or do I obey and go into the unknown.

There's no mention of any prophetic reference to Elisha's life before Elijah appears.

In a decision to obey the voice of God, he moves from plowboy to spiritual son to prophet.

My spiritual son, Todd Williams called me soon after he recognized me as his father.

He told me that after years and years of doing ministry (plowing his field) that he would need to follow Elisha's example.

Elisha was a man of order and honor. He served his natural father with his twelve yokes of oxen (twelve represent order or government).

To receive the new mantle of a spiritual father, he would take his old "servant mindset" and dismantle the old yoke, sacrifice the oxen and use the wood of the yoke as an altar of fire.

Todd dismantled his ministry.

He embraced the new season, impartation and mantle.

Todd understood that once you kill the Ox you can't go back.

Obedience is significant for every son in this season.

Elisha transitions from a servant to a son.

Elisha never leaves Elijah for eighteen years.

Elijah is desiring to go to Bethel and say goodbye to those in the school of prophets. He tells Elisha to stay in Gilgal but Elisha responds:

And Elijah said to Elisha, "Stay here, for the Lord

has told me to go to Bethel." But Elisha replied, "As surely as the Lord lives and you yourself live, I will never leave you!" So, they went down together to Bethel. 2Kings 2:2

There is a reward for obedience.

Elijah talks to his son Elisha as he faces his last moments on earth.

And so, it was, when they had crossed over, that Elijah said to Elisha, "Ask! What may I do for you, before I am taken away from you?"

Elisha said, "Please let a double portion of your spirit be upon me."

So, he said, "You have asked a hard thing. Nevertheless, if you see me when I am taken from you, it shall be so for you; but if not, it shall not be so." Then it happened, as they continued on and talked, that suddenly a chariot of fire appeared with horses of fire, and separated the two of them; and Elijah went up by a whirlwind into heaven.

*And Elisha saw it, and he cried out, "**My father, my father,** the chariot of Israel and its horsemen!" So, he saw him no more.* 2 Kings 2:9-12

Your greatest experiences come from being a son.

Your greatest rewards come from being an obedient son.

Todd and April have left the old wine skin of personalities, pressure and performance. They no longer lead a church but a family. They share how they have discovered a certain satisfaction and confidence that comes when you embrace sonship, where before they were an isolated servant.

The world and especially the "Church" world are filled with men and women who are "wearied from well-doing." Some are ready to do about anything but ministry, in order to save their marriage and family.

I want you to know that this New Season brings new hope.

The world is suffering from a fatherless earth.

We desperately need fathers.

To be a good father, you must first be a good son.

A good and obedient son.

NOTES

CHAPTER EIGHT

A SEASON OF ORDER

As stated earlier, every move of God has a purpose:

- To recover biblical truth.
- God is the God of order.
- There is a specific pattern and order to the things of God.

That which was lost was replaced with religious identity. Which resulted in disorder and dysfunction. Alterations and adaptations have been made to Christ's Church to be more acceptable to the orphan mindset.

With our identity compromised we must change not only our mindset but the model. Reform is defined, "to bring back to original intent." Therefore, Apostolic Reformation is to bring back authentic Christianity like experienced in the Acts of the Apostles.

In other words, let's rediscover the success formula of the early church.

Anything that the Holy Spirit did not construct or blueprint for His Church through the scriptures we must destruct in order to restructure or reform so we are totally committed to the manual written by the Designer.

Having planted many, many churches over the years, I understand easily the traditions of men, cultural compromise and superstition can permeate and penetrate the purist filter.

God has always placed a leader or a Set Man over a group of sons.

It's the order of God.

The anointing God placed upon Moses, he placed on 70 delegated to reproduce himself.

Jesus, the Son of God, fathered twelve sons.

The Apostle Paul was concerned about the seacoast family in Corinth.

*Even if you had ten thousand guardians in Christ, you do not have many **fathers**, for in Christ Jesus **I became your father** through the gospel.* 1 Corinthians 4:15 NIV

Paul told Timothy that there is an effective way to lead and father.

*And the things that you have heard from **me** among many witnesses, commit these to **faithful men** who will be able to teach **others** also.* 2 Timothy 2:2

This is Apostolic Succession of Four Generations:

1. Paul 2. Timothy 3. Faithful Men 4. Others.

Fathers and sons move the message and wineskin generationally.

One of the most important aspect of this New Season of Sons is the Apostles doctrine – solid teaching that establishes the family of God in the Household of Faith.

Flaky, fleshly and the latest fad preaching have produced fractious, foolish, immature sons operating in "strange fire."

Aaron was sacrificing per God's instructions at the first tabernacle (Leviticus 8—9). One day, two of Aaron's sons, Nadab and Abihu, came along and offered incense with "strange fire." The Hebrew word translated "strange" means "**unauthorized, foreign,** or **profane.**" God not only rejected their sacrifice; He found it so offensive that He consumed the two men with fire.

Since it was the fire that was unauthorized, it could be that Nadab and Abihu were burning the incense **with fire of their own making** rather than taking fire from the altar, as specified in Leviticus 19:12.

In Acts 5:1–11, a husband and wife lied to Peter about land given to the church, and they were judged with physical death because of their deception.

As Peter puts it,

"Why have you conceived this thing in your heart? You have not lied just to men but to God" Acts 5:4.

The God of the Old Covenant is the God of the New Covenant.

The deception, disrespect and dishonor of Aaron's sons, and of the couple who lied to Apostle Peter, were their downfall.

Attention to order and accuracy to the pattern of God does not change.

Nor did the outcome to those who violated it out of rebellion and disorder.

In this New Season, God is restoring order!

Fathers are leading the house once again.

And he will turn the hearts of the fathers to the children, And the hearts of the children to their fathers, Lest I come and strike the earth with a curse. Malachi 4:6

Disorder, dysfunction and disunity are evident in both the natural and spiritual family on earth. With the father of the house set in place, order and alignment are restored. Sons will be established and truth that has been lost will be recovered.

Stop praying for a reviving of the disorder and an old wineskin.

Reformation is required.

When Martin Luther produced his ninety-five theses in 1517 and placed them on the doors of the churches, great social and political changes resulted throughout Europe. The old order removed Luther from his post as professor at the University of Wittenberg and excommunicated him from the church.

But a New Season was born.

The picture of Jesus in Revelation 3;20 standing and knocking at a door is shocking.

He is outside His Church!

Revelation 3:20 is Christ's letter to the church at Laodicea—also known as the lukewarm church. In Revelation 3:14-22, the Lord condemns them for their spiritual self-deception and apathy. Christ says, "I know your deeds, that you are neither cold nor hot; I wish that you were cold or hot." They exhibited no spiritual zeal or authentic love for God or His Word. They professed to know Christ, but He had no place in their gathering.

Disorder, not a strategy of hell, has placed Christ outside His Church.

In this New Season sons must see the four pillars (Acts 2:42) of the New Testament church and restore the family of God back to proper order, purpose and function.

NOTES

CHAPTER NINE
A SEASON OF GREAT OPPORTUNITY

An opportunity is an invitation to an experience.

The contemporary church plays it safe. Status quo, same old same old.

Recycled sermons to overly sensitive, satisfied saints.

How boring!

In this New Season of sons, the word is: Opportunity.

It was the secret of the Early Church.

They didn't sit around waiting for something to happen.

They were in the middle of what was happening.

Despite early persecution of Christians under the Roman Empire, Christianity expanded throughout the world.

How?

They embraced opportunity.

1. Established the new converts in the Apostle's Doctrine.

2. Traveled from Jerusalem starting new works

3. Spoke boldly wherever they went.

So, they called them and commanded them not to speak at all nor teach in the name of Jesus. But Peter and John answered and said to them, "Whether it is right in the sight of God to listen to you more than to God, you judge. For we cannot but speak the things which we have seen and heard." Acts 3:18-20

Opportunity can be lost through doublemindedness, disagreement and disobedience.

Paul knew his son Timothy.

He was confident that his son would not miss his opportunity.

When I call to remembrance the genuine faith that is in you, which dwelt first in your grandmother Lois and your mother Eunice, and I am persuaded is in you also. Therefore, I remind you to **stir up the gift** *of God which is in you through the* **laying on of my hands.***For God has not given us a spirit of fear, but of power and of love and of a sound mind.* 2 Timothy 2:5-7

After the Book of Acts the word, "Disciple" is no longer used.

The Apostle Paul recognized sons, family and households of faith.

Early Christians viewed the church as a family. They saw themselves as brothers and sisters and mothers and fathers to everyone who was part of the Christian community.

"Church" wasn't a building

The first church buildings did not start to appear until early 200AD. The Apostle Paul blew open the doors of the home and welcomed in all believers as brothers and sisters. He created a new focus on the family that extended far beyond one's nuclear relatives and included people of every race and social strata who gave their allegiance to the risen Christ.

The great opportunity for a reforming of a new wineskin is upon us.

This is the season to seize the opportunity of recovering the lost truth of God's family.

Never forget, the family was God's idea.

God saw the earth was out of order, He desired to have a family on earth to set things in order.

He sowed His Son and He reaped a Family.

A spiritual family led by a spiritual father will have favor, influence and a future.

FOUR TRAITS OF A GOOD FAMILY MEMBER

1. A TONGUE THAT HONORS

Rom.13:7 Give honor where it is due.

Eph.6:2-3 Honor your father & mother and live a longer life.

Prov.15:33 Before Honor comes humility.

Prov.11:16 A gracious woman obtains honor.

Prov. 22:4 The reward of humility & reverence of the Lord are riches, honor & life.

2. A TENDER HEART

Eph.4:32 Be kind, tender hearted, forgiving

James 1:19 Quick to hear, slow to speak and slow to anger.

Hardness of heart leads to Hardheadedness.

3. A TELLER OF TRUTH

John 8:32 Truth Seekers are free people.

Prov. 12:19 Truthful lips endure forever, lying tongue is momentary.

Prov.28:13 Whoever conceals his sin shall not prosper but he who confesses and forsakes them will obtain mercy.

4. A TEACHABLE SPIRIT

Prov. 13:18 Poverty & shame come to him who ignores instruction.

Prov.9:9 Give instruction to a wise man and he will be wiser.

Prov. 12:2 Whoever loves discipline loves knowledge, but he who hates correction is stupid.

Touchy people are unteachable and if they are unteachable, they are uncorrectable.

This is season of opportunity for sons to discover a family without fear. 1 John 4:8

A place of Correction that creates Direction.

Direction that provides Protection and Opportunity.

NOTES

CHAPTER TEN

THE SEASON OF HONOR

The DNA of the Kingdom is honor.

This is a truth that God is restoring in this Season.

Our culture is imploding from dishonor.

Dishonor is rapid from the school house, the White House and the Church house.

It is shaping and giving voice to a generation of entitled and self- absorbed thinking individuals.

Some years ago, in the USA, a card company created, "Clergy Appreciation Month." A time each October when Churches were to honor their pastor.

Can you believe a card company had to remind people to honor their spiritual leader?

We are taught in Romans 13:7 to give honor, where honor is due.

In many places it is long overdue!

In the conventional church honor is out of obligation. (It is Clergy Appreciation Day). One Sunday each year is set aside to recognize the church leader.

In a Spiritual family with a Spiritual father honor is reciprocation.

As the father of the Household of Faith, my sons are taught honor 365 days a year. Honor is the currency of the Kingdom. When you teach sons honor, you have provided a right foundation for life, relationships and Kingdom life.

Respect is an attitude.

Honor is a decision.

Honor is a demonstration.

Honor is the seed for access. Access is the key to success.

Honor makes you unforgettable and so does dishonor.

How do you show honor?

Embrace your divine role in the family as a son.

How do you show Dishonor?

Disregard an instruction of your father.

Show disinterest. Never call, contact, participate or be available.

Be unthankful. Your ability to communicate gratitude is very important.

Dishonor creates disconnection in every relationship.

Noah had three sons, Shem, Ham, and Japheth.

In Genesis 9:20-27 after the flood, Noah planted a vineyard, he drank the wine, became drunk and he laid uncovered in his tent.

Ham dishonored his father by viewing the nakedness of Noah. The word "nakedness" refers to "intimacy." Ham exposed his father in a vulnerable, intimate moment.

We understand God chose Noah to fulfill a great assignment on the earth.

We also understand fathers are from perfect.

Upon hearing what Ham had done, Shem and Japheth take a blanket and walk backwards to cover their father.

When Noah learns of Ham's actions, he curses him. Which generationally produced two groups from Ham's offspring: Egyptians and Canaanites. Two groups that God's people had to be delivered from and conquer.

Dishonor has generational consequences.

NOTES

TEN THOUGHTS ABOUT HONOR FOR SONS

1. Honor is shown through learning and serving. Jesus honored His earthly father, Joseph.

2. Honor will cause you to emerge from behind those you've served, without eclipsing who you've served.

3. Honor means I'm respecting what I'm becoming – maturing son - father

4. What you Honor, you attract. What you dishonor, you forfeit.

5. Refusing to Honor the father you have chosen, means you think little of yourself. If they're not worthy of honor, why are they leading you?

6. Sons, fathers need your strength. You need a father's wisdom. Reciprocal Honor creates an unbreakable bond. Seek covering son.

7. When your father bestows Honor on you, don't become prideful. Pride is an honor extinguisher. Stay humble and Honor will seek you out.

8. Honor God with your finances. "Honor the Lord with thy substance and with the first fruits of increase" Proverbs 3:9. When you withhold the tithe, you have dishonored the instruction of God.

9. No matter how right you think you are, if you won't Honor God by following basic instructions from your father, Honor will elude you.

10. Honor is not an event but a lifestyle.

DR. PAUL CRITES

- Delivered his first public message at age 20 in 1978.

- Graduate of Southeastern University in Lakeland, Florida and Logos Graduate School in Jacksonville, Florida.

- Embraced his assignment to empower and mentor over two million people from over forty nations through personal appearances and video training programs.

- Author of many celebrated books and training resources.

- Founder of Destiny Christian College in 1987, now New Covenant University with thousands of graduates serving throughout the world.

- Recognized for his international service for his work with the nation of South Africa by then Ambassador Dr. Piet Koornhof during the nation's critical transition of power.

- Established Purpose International in 1998, a 501-c-3 ministry organization to train leaders and assist in humanitarian outreach.

- Ordained as a Bishop by The College of Bishops in 2003, he provides covering and care for ministers in the USA and internationally.

- Traveled and served as a part of a delegation of American Leaders for Middle East Peace.

- Founder, Apostle of My Wisdom Center, a Household of Faith in St. Augustine, Florida.

- Happily married to Dr. Angel Crites, they have six children and three grands.

- His dog is named, Elvis

For more information

PaulCrites.com